Even When

Julie Brown

ISBN: 978-1-956654-80-6

Acknowledgments:

First and foremost, to God who saved me and gave me the gift of writing. I will always honor You.

To my family who always answered my calls, read the roughest of drafts, and allowed me to do what I love.

To the posse, my friends from all stages of life (you know who you are), and to everyone mentioned in this book, you are always the iron that sharpens iron. Thank you for allowing God to work through you to touch my life.

To Cynthia Hickey who made this book come alive.

EVEN WHEN

I'm a Christian suspense fiction writer. I like the mystery/suspense genres because it keeps me guessing and thinking. Can I solve the problems and mysteries surrounding my characters in 100,000 words or less? I love the fiction aspect because I can make up any character I want, they will do what I say, and I can predict and set to words the exact outcome I want. I write Christian fiction because God gave me a gift and who am I not to honor the Giver with the talents He's placed in me?

When my husband, Dennis and I were standing in front of our family and friends at our wedding, we said we'd love each other forever. I thought that I had a life-long partner, and we would grow old together. Dennis was diagnosed in 2018 with throat cancer and we both believed up until the last couple of months of his life that God would grant us a miracle. We could go back to "normal". "Normal" used to mean planning things like vacations, and socially interacting with family and friends, not keeping a "go-bag" ready.

Physical healing was a possibility for our great, big God, wasn't it? Yes, it was, just in a different form than either of us wanted or thought possible. I constantly caught myself saying things like "If only you'll do this…I'll do this" or "Your will is all we want". The first was just a desperate barter, the second conflicted with the first. Both were attempts to control the situation and then maybe release it back to God. An ugly tug-of-war that left me exhausted. I couldn't barter with God and I didn't fully believe that His will would include Dennis dying. Why couldn't the characters in my life story just do what I wanted? Why couldn't I control my life and my husband's life like I could with my fictional characters?

So during that three year period after the diagnosis, I did what I was raised to do. I prayed. Prayed to the Giver of Life, to the God whom my parents trusted and who raised me to trust. Several of my close friends (I call them my posse) always say "Fake it until you make it." Well, I faked it on many days, days that I worked long hours to make up for lost time spent caretaking, days that I took him to treatment, days that we received bad news from reports, and even on days where everything felt normal. "Faking it" really wasn't what was happening, more like I was trying not to break down every five minutes.

My gracious family and friends were compassionate when I did lose it. I was desperately trying to make my physical and emotional being match up to my spiritual one. My favorite phrases during that time were "God's got this" and "I will be faithful because God has been faithful to me". Saying (faking) those words until I believed (made it) was what kept me going.

I'm now a widow. Dennis, just shy of our 24th wedding anniversary, passed away in March 2021. I would never have written being a widow at 54 years of age into my story. Losing a spouse to death is so very different than losing a child or a parent or a friend. The grief and loss will come to all of those situations the same, but as a dear friend who lost his wife said, "losing a child is like losing the future, losing a parent is like losing the past, and losing your spouse is like losing your present."

In all grief and sorrow, your foundation is rocked and sometimes crushed. Only by standing and trusting the promises that the living God has written in His Word can we emerge from this devastation and live. I tell the kids in our youth group that Dennis' story is fulfilled; he's rejoicing in Heaven at the feet of Jesus. But my story is not yet complete. And to plant my feet and say "I'm going to make it through" can only be accomplished by letting the Author of my soul take over and write the rest of my story.

The promises in this book are just reminders of what God has already promised for you, the broken-hearted, grief-stricken, heavy-laden people who trust God. I write what I know so there will be many instances/stories that relate to being a widow, but as another dear friend texted me one day "God sees you" in all of your circumstances and He wants you to take these promises, dwell on them, shove them under your "foundation", write them on your walls, let them soak in.

He really does see you. Knows you by name. Loves you beyond what you can even imagine.

Psalm 23 has been a foundational collection of verses for me during this time of grieving and God has pulled out different sections, whispered in my ear, sometimes invaded my dreams, and highlighted what He wanted me to get out of each verse. And like any good writer, He outlined them and said "stay home and write". Share them with people, tell them the good news…SO…

In every part of my life—physically, relationally/emotionally, financially, and spiritually-God is…

My Provider

My Protector

My Planner

Psalm 23 the Passion translation (tPt)

1 Yahweh is my best friend and my shepherd.

I always have more than enough.

2 He offers a resting place for me in his luxurious

love. His tracks take me to an oasis of peace

near the quiet brook of bliss.

3 That's where he restores and revives my life.

He opens before me the right path and leads

me along in his footsteps of righteousness so

that I can bring honor to his name.

4 Even when your path takes me through the valley

of deepest darkness, fear will never conquer me,

for you already have! Your authority is my

strength and my peace. The comfort of your

love takes away my fear. I'll never be lonely,

for you are near.

5 You become my delicious feast even when my

enemies dare to fight. You anoint me with the

fragrance of your Holy Spirit; you give me all I

can drink of you until my cup overflows.

6 So why would I fear the future? Only goodness

and tender love pursue me all the days of my

life. Then afterward, when my life is through,
I'll return to your glorious presence to be
forever with you!

SECTION ONE-God is my PROVIDER

Yahweh is my best friend and my shepherd; I always have more than enough. Psalm 23:1 (tPt)

You anoint me with the fragrance of your Holy Spirit; you give me all I can drink of you until my cup overflows. Psalm 23:5b (tPt)

Chapter One- God is my provider physically

I have always been self-sufficient. Even as a child, I knew what I wanted and could/would make it happen. This was usually the source of conflict with my dad who wanted me to do what he wanted (of course, since he was my parent). Now, I would call that rebellion, with always a means to an end.

My life at home with my parents and siblings was largely uneventful except for the heated arguments with my dad and my un-Christian like behavior. I was raised to go to church, be kind to people, love your family and God, and serve each other. That lifestyle didn't really suite me as it left ME out of the equation. I had plans. And I wasn't afraid to buck the system in place at home to get me to those plans. I could handle myself and didn't really need the protection offered by my parents or ultimately, God.

I attended a Youth for Christ camp for several summers and decided that the right thing to do (after all, I was serving at church so I might as well make it official) was accept Jesus as my Lord and Savior. I was serious about my commitment to God as long as He went along with my plans. My mom used to say "I've got angels watching over you" to which I would reply in my head "Well, they'd better turn their back" because I was doing it. Whatever "it" was that I wanted to do. I had an amazing youth pastor, an incredibly Godly lead pastor, and parents who loved Jesus. It was me and my rebellion that separated me from God and the church.

When I was a young teenager, a friend and I would ride our horses over to a small arena and hang out for the day. This was obviously a long time ago when children were allowed to play outside for hours and only checked in at supper time. My route to the arena took me across a country highway, five miles down a gravel road, and to the edge of a little town. The whole ride there and back, I would make up stories about a handsome cowboy that I would meet (after I was a famous writer and had successfully accomplished a career), marry, and live happily ever after.

That was my "want" list…and I had every intention of getting what I wanted. Over the years and through several failed relationships (one of which he proposed to me on stage in front of 1000 youth only to say he was just kidding after the concert was over), I changed and added to that husband "want" list to fit who I was dating at the time.

I went to college as soon as I graduated from high school, lived off-campus my sophomore through senior year, and generally was able to maintain a self-sufficient life. My senior year, I lived with a 93-year-old, sweet lady who let me live in her house rent free as long as I took her to the hair salon and grocery store on Saturdays. See? Means to an end.

Fast forward a couple of years to my first real job, a case manager at a correctional facility in northern Missouri. During college, I swung back and forth between a sold-out Christian and a self-seeking rebel, hell-bent (literally) on destroying my foundational roots and grounding in the church. The prison job reinforced my need to provide for myself; it was a very dark time in my life. Mostly because of the atmosphere of desperation and lack of hope, but also because I learned the dark side of people was way more than I had ever experienced.

People were cruel, unkind, greedy, powerful, and had no desire to see you succeed unless it meant their own success as well. And that was the staff. To stay self-sufficient, I submerged myself in that culture and completely lost sight of that little rebellious girl that sang "Jesus wants me as a sunbeam" while kissing boys in the church basement. Not just lost sight, but buried her deep.

Tragedy often brings us back to our roots and I experienced a lot in a couple of short years: one of my closest friends passed away, my grandmother passed away, I got snared in a sexual harassment case involving a supervisor (he was walked out of the prison a year later in handcuffs on felony charges), and the guy I was dating went back to a former relationship.

I was devastated and decidedly not self-reliant. I knew my foundation. So I went back to church.

"Come to me all who are weary and heavy-laden, and I will give you rest." Matthew 11:28

All of the above happened before I was 25. I was tired. Exhausted. And clearly, not able to take care of myself based on my track record. After all of the tragedies happened, I was in my car going to a different job and there was an accident in front of me. A bad one. I watched the fire department pull this young driver out of his car and load him on the stretcher and all I could think about was "it must be nice to not have to think for a while". Those were truly my thoughts. Because of the things I'd been through, I wanted to change places with that severely injured kid?! Because I was done. Done trying to "handle" everything. Done trying to make things happen.

I knew my foundation; I knew what to do when I was at the end of me. I called up the local church and said, "I need help". Some of the hardest words I'd ever spoken. They welcomed me in, and I went to the altar at the first chance and recommitted my life. I needed that "rest" that I knew would only come when I got right with Jesus. My body physically needed that promised rest.

"Fear not, you are more valuable than the sparrows." Luke 12:7

Someone spoke that verse over me after I came back to the church. Probably because I doubted that God would redeem the time I spent away from Him and there must be a time of consequences coming. But the verse doesn't say NOW you are more valuable than the sparrows, now that you've come back, now that you are serving me. It just says "YOU ARE"...present tense, no qualifiers. And the sparrows? According to the identification bird books, sparrows are problem-causers (hmmm…) who compete for nesting sites, take over food sources, and crowd out less aggressive birds from traditional ranges and habitats. (https://www.thespruce.com/ discouraging-house-sparrows-386419). Again, hmmm, sound familiar? Like maybe that was me? And I'm more valuable than the sparrows. Time to change perspective.

At the church that I was attending, I ran into Mr. Right. And married him. On our honeymoon, I gave him a small notebook that I'd been writing in since those trips to the arena. My ever-changing list of Mr Right qualities was in that notebook. At the top of the list, I had recently added: #1 Must love Jesus more than me. Things listed under the #1 were: must have a house and the same job for more than five years (shows stability), must be able to cook (because I can't), must have a fenced-in yard (for our dogs), must have blue eyes and dark hair, and must be taller than me. Quite a list. Do you know that my husband matched every single one of those things? And more. More physical, spiritual, and relational attributes than I had listed or even knew that I wanted. But God did. And He caused "my cup to overflow" with His goodness. He said I was more valuable than the sparrows and proved it by overwhelming me with His wants for me. I only had to turn to Him and get out of my own way.

"And we know that for those who love God, all things work together for good for those who are called according to His purpose." Romans 8:28

As I write this book, I am constantly reminded of how good God is to me. Every one of His promises are true EVEN WHEN you don't see the physical protection. God says in His Word that you are more valuable than the sparrows, do you believe that? Do you need to change your perspective on how He feels about you and how He continues to provide? I encourage you to list the ways below that God has provided for you physically and use it as a reminder for you in the days to come:

EVEN WHEN

Chapter Two- God is my provider relationally/emotionally

"Abraham called that place 'the Lord will Provide'" Genesis 22:14

You've probably heard this story... Abraham was told by God to bring his one and only son to the mountain to become a burnt offering. Just that sentence makes me cringe. Somewhere between verse two (where God told Abraham what to do) and verse three (Abraham loaded his donkey with wood and instructed his son to come with him), there had to be a lot of mental turmoil for Abraham. "Why?" or "Why him and not me?" or my probable question "Is that really you, God?" But he did it, because he trusted God. Even Isaac questioned his father ("Where is the lamb for the offering?"), and still, still he allowed Abraham to bind him up and lay him down on top of the altar over the wood. I'm sure Isaac could have overpowered Abraham but instead he was compliant because he trusted his father. And just before the death blow, the angel of the Lord stopped him and provided a burnt offering through a ram that just happened to be nearby, stuck in a thicket. Just so happened to show up.

See the triangle? Abraham trusted his relationship with God, Isaac trusted his relationship with his father which made him also trust God who spared his life and provided. God already knew what was going to happen, but these relationships built on trust caused Abraham and Isaac both to share what God had done by building an altar and naming it "the Lord will provide".

"He who did not spare His own son, but gave him up for us all- how will He not also, along with him, graciously give us all things?"

Romans 8:32

(God referring to his own son, Jesus)

Although I have built a lot of unhealthy relationships over the years, I can fully say that I now have the best friends' base of anyone I know. I can identify when each came into my life, how long they stayed, and if there was a purpose to their time in my life. My life-long friend from the sixth grade is still my friend- she walked with me through some of the rebellion times always saying, "I'm not sure we should be doing this." I met my husband in a great group of singles, who are mostly married now, but still friends. My siblings and their families and their spouses' families are friends.

We had couples friends to do life with who had children the same age as our son. A daughter-in-law and her family who always include me. I walked through a very successful, 15-year career, making hundreds of friends with the students, their parents, the administration/staff, and the board of education. Out of those hundreds, a core group of friends (the 'posse') developed that have been my heartbeat on more than one occasion. The next major career move brought many other dear people into my life.

The friendships God has blessed me with through several different churches has been just right. Right timing, right love for each other, incredible mentors and all blessings.

God also designed us with emotions. Some of us are better at expressing them than others and some of us need a little time to trust others with those emotions. I had a boss (who is now part of that posse) that continually said to me "I can't tell what you're thinking by your face." Well, I'd learned the poker face from working at the prison where I bluffed my way through and never allowed anyone to know what I was thinking. It took a while, but I learned to "fix my face" or at least show some kind of emotion. God provided me with "safe" people to share my emotions with who would help me see the balance between my emotions (feelings) and truth.

"For the Lord God is brighter than the brilliance of a sunrise! Wrapping himself around me like a shield, he is so generous with his gifts of grace and glory. Those who walk along his paths

with integrity will never lack one thing they need,
for he provides it all!" Psalm 84:11

God knew exactly when I was going to need each of those friends and provided the groundwork for beautiful relationships. When Dennis became sick, I needed every single one of those people in my life. They wrote cards, gave us rides to treatment, sent meals, sat with us through horrible diagnoses, helped me navigate the ugly waters of death, and loved on me in ways that I didn't even know I needed (like neighbors and men from the church taking care of things around the house/yard).

Through each of these relationships, God has displayed His love for me and provided...every single time.

I know that God has provided relationships that drive you closer to Him, that sharpen you and make you a better person, the ones that are soul-driven and life-long. EVEN WHEN it doesn't feel like you belong or that you have any close friends, God is working in the background, positioning people to come alongside you. In the space below, list the relationships that God has interwoven in your life and use these as reminders of how God provides relationally and emotionally.

Chapter Three- God is my provider financially

I am not a shopper. I am not a "watch for the sales" person. I am not a coupon-er. Side note: I found it fun to neatly cut out coupons on everything, even those things that I cared less about, put them in nice piles according to category and then...throw them up in the air and watch them scatter to all sides of the room, under the couch, over the dog. Extremely satisfying and a stress reliever. I did the exact same thing with glass bottles- drank whatever was in them only to use them for target practice later. That glorious sound of glass breaking at my hands and without anyone's head smashed in the process. I didn't skimp on these activities or think of them as a waste.

Back to the shopping... Dennis was a shopper.

He shopped for quality, one-of-a-kind items, or ones that gave him the most bang for his buck. He loved to go to auctions and estate sales. I'd go with him to the estate sales, but the gun and farm auctions, he always had a close friend with him.

This close friend and I had an understanding: if it wasn't necessary, please talk him out of it. On the one occasion that this friend failed me (not really, but we tease about it), the two of them went to an auction with the hopes of bringing home a most sought-after gun that Dennis had been looking for. With my friend's wife and I crafting, it was a pleasant day until the guys got home. I was outside spray painting something and I saw the truck come around the corner with a small boat attached. I waited until they had parked and then looked at my friend with raised eyebrows. I hadn't even looked at my husband yet. "I just went to the restroom" he said as he went to greet his wife in the house. What ensued was a very long conversation (not really two-sided) about why we needed a boat.

The one thing Dennis always fell back on was

the money he was spending was from cash awards from work. He worked for a business for over forty years and was highly acclaimed for not only his work ethic, but his ability to spin something from nothing for a fraction of the cost which gained him many cash awards for his cost savings projects. The money he spent on anything I probably wouldn't have agreed to spending (or he hadn't discussed with me) was simply "extra" that didn't take away from the household expenses or our way of living. Which is how the various tattoos came about and why I now have a very extensive record album collection and three record players for each of the rooms he spent time in. And, also, why I let him live, just kidding; he got enjoyment out of the things that he really wanted.

Because my husband was older than me by about 15 years, he would hit retirement age before me. He always said that it worked out perfectly because I had another 10 years or so of working in me so he'd just be a houseboy, cooking and cleaning for the rest of his days. Of all the things he's been involved with over the years- knife making, gun collecting, tae kwon do, lapidary, hunting, camping, kickboxing, just to name a few- I doubted he would just be a houseboy. I knew he had been saving money through his paycheck for that eventual day because I did all of the check-writing, bill-paying, balancing accounts, and general bookkeeping. I also knew the expenses we had: the mortgage, the vehicles, the Christian school tuition, the credit card balances.

> *"And God is able to bless you abundantly, so that in all things,*
> *at all times having all that you need, you will abound in every good work."* 2 Cor 9:8

Dennis also loved to bless people out of the abundance of his cash awards and the other over-and-above money that God had blessed us with. He loved to pay a student's way to a youth event or give to a cause or give one of his guns away just simply because God had blessed him. My dad commented that he would love to get his hands on a replica gun that he used in the Marines; my husband heard that "want" and searched high and low for the gun. He gave it to him as a surprise one day with the thought that God had blessed him with the right gun at the right price and at the right time. Although Dennis was a wizard at making things happen financially, he was always quick to say he was only passing on the blessing. God granted him with a quick mind, coupled with compassion and an open hand.

I was always provided for and our *needs* as a family were met. There were "priority" *wants*, like a Christian school education, that God provided an abundance for at just the right time. The surprise raise at the time property tax was due or the unexpected check in the mail just when our refrigerator died. The blessings didn't always come financially, but when they did, it felt like reassurance that God knows and cares about us, the Brown family.

This isn't saying we had it all together

financially all the time, BUT we believed in this promise and cheerfully gave to others because we knew (trusted) that God would provide for us. We were firm believers in tithing which goes hand in hand with this promise.

If you unpack the verse above, He says "ALL" three times in one sentence. All things, at all times having all that you need- pretty self-explanatory. But look at the verbs...God is...you will... present and future tense.

After Dennis passed away, I had a lot of questions, naturally. Most were spiritual and emotional, but some were physical and financial. I was asked on more than one occasion if I was moving. That one surprised me...was I supposed to? Is that what widows did? Move out of the home where so many memories had been made? I dealt with so many insurance companies, doctors and hospitals, my husband's workplace, this representative and that one in those first months. I spent countless lunch breaks talking to necessary individuals, telling them over and over again that I was reporting my husband as deceased. Hours asking the same questions: "what are the next steps? Who do I talk to now? Explain this to me again. I have to change all of the beneficiaries that we had just set up and all of the emergency contacts?" I mentioned in the second chapter that God provided so many friends and family that came alongside me and gave advice. And I took their advice and used the people they recommended and prayed each day. "Give me grace, Lord, to make the right decisions." He is able. "You are able."

We had three vehicles, a house, countless medical bills, and I now had to think about moving? People continually said to me "You don't have to do everything at once. You can go slow." Well, I don't think some of those people had ever been through the process of declaring their spouse as deceased, despite their well-meaning comments and their love for me. The call to Social Security caused a lot of accounts (including credit cards) to be closed so there wasn't any fraudulent activity and if you weren't the main person on accounts (like the cell phones), they wouldn't even talk with you until you've jumped through the proper hoops (sending the death certificate). Or the contracts that have your name on them, but you aren't the policyholder (like the mortgage or the vehicle registration).

The first big financial hit after my husband's death came through the funeral home. Dennis had his whole funeral planned out several years ago after the diagnosis (as did I) and I fulfilled his wishes completely with the program and the picture he wanted used right down to the person he wanted to sing at the service. Even knowing all of that information, I was shocked at the expense and the need for payment immediately before the funeral (within a week's time). I suppose this was normal, but I'd never been on this end before. My friends jumped in and made the flower arrangement, manned the guest book, sat with me while I tried to stay upright and just breathe. My pastor and his wife walked me through every step from the entering of hospice to long after the funeral. My family and my daughter-in-law's family and

Dennis' family supported me in ways that I probably haven't even realized yet.

And through it all, God was in the details and knew my husband's time on earth was over. Several years ago, I started squirreling away money from different things and was well on the way to surprising my husband with the trip he'd always wanted: to see Alaska. I'd planned it for our 25th wedding anniversary. When Dennis died two months before our 24th anniversary, do you know how much money I had in a savings account? Enough to pay for the funeral that he wanted.

So, I ask again, "I'm supposed to move?"

"Well, can you afford to stay?"

Oh.

I'd seen everything God had done in preparation for this day. Here was yet another question that I didn't know the answer to or was even capable of thinking about. So, God in all of his glory, took it out of my hands. He brought in friends of my husband's that had become my friends and reminded me of another friend who handled financial things and I sought their counsel. To this day, I will always remember standing in the driveway opening another envelope addressed to the "spouse of..." and discovering that the pension I would be receiving for the rest of my life was $20 more than the mortgage. I was stunned and burst into tears in my driveway, awed by a God that cared about me and my finances and was preparing a way before I was ever born.

"First He supplies every need plus more.
Then He multiplies the seed as you sow it, so
that the harvest of your generosity will grow.
You will be abundantly enriched in every way as
you give generously in every way (on every
occasion) for when we take these gifts to those in
need it causes many to give thanks to God."
2 Corinthians 9:10b-11

The last part of that verse "it causes many to give thanks to God" are an indication of your next steps. Make sure you give God the glory. When I tell that story, I always follow up with "that's my God story". Even to my friends who aren't believers. Because I want everyone to know Who provided for me, Who cares about me above all, and Who cares about them, too. He is…and you will…

In the space below, list the ways God has abundantly blessed you financially. If you're in a spot where you can't see that yet, write the verses in this chapter out on notecards and pray over them daily. If you are tithing, I promise you, the blessings are on the way. In the right way at the right time, which is the only way He does things. If you aren't tithing, I would encourage you to watch my pastor's series on tithing and let Him who loves you speak to you through His word. (YouTube- FWC Smithville, The Blessed Life Series based on the book and sermon series by Robert Morris of Gateway Church) EVEN WHEN the finances aren't there or you're worried about bills and debt and the list could go on and on, but EVEN WHEN all these things are in your face, He promises to provide for you.

Chapter Four- God is my provider spiritually

Earlier in the book, I mentioned that I grew up in a Christian home surrounded by Godly people: my parents, my youth pastor, my parents' church friends, my friends' and their families, even my extended family (aunts and uncles and cousins). I had every example possible to lead me on the straight and narrow. But I chose differently. I chose to ignore my parents' warnings; I chose to ignore the God who loved me and instead, looked for ways to put a damper on the plan He had for me. I allowed the enemy into my life and only turned to God when it was convenient.

"The thief comes only to steal, kill, and destroy. I have come that they may have life and have it to the full." John 10:10

When my parents moved to the country so they could have a farm and I could have a horse, I decided to be mad at the world because they moved me away from my friends. I was only 11 years old, but that seemed to be the start of my spiraling. The enemy stole some very important time from me during my junior high and high school years. Because I let him. He tried to kill my relationship with my parents, my biggest protectors, mentors, and faithful supporters. Because I let him.

I knew the truth. I knew God would always be there…isn't that what He promised? But I chose to slide out from under that umbrella of truth and do things my way.

Doing things my way meant almost putting myself in a dysfunctional relationship.

Doing things my way meant running fast and loose with a couple of drug dealers and almost going to jail. The cops had been watching these two for several days and scooped them up the morning after I had been out joyriding with them. The police had to have seen me on surveillance.

Doing things my way meant bringing home scumbags to my parent's house just to get a rise out of them.

Doing things my way meant thinking I was "all that" when a fight broke out in the prison yard and I was later told it was just a distraction and the main reason for the fight was to kidnap a female worker and set off a riot.

Doing things my way meant a lot of heartache, a lot of damage, and allowing the enemy a seat at whatever table, couch, or bed was available. I should have been dead, pregnant, or spending time in prison. Oh, but for the grace of God. Even when I was off doing my own thing, I believe that the prayers of my parents created a covering or hedge around me so that none of those things happened.

I always tell parents who have struggling, rebellious children, to continue to pray. Lay the foundation (Proverbs 22:6) and they'll return to it. Always cover your children in prayer even when they completely disregard you and your words.

When I came back to the church and Dennis and I began to date, we had so many other couples who spoke into our lives. I became involved with a Bible study with other women who were just beyond me in years. While I was pregnant with our son, they had toddlers. When our son was a toddler, theirs were in elementary. Not only were they one step "above" me in their family lives, but also spiritually. I soaked up everything they gave me, thoughts on raising Godly children, advice on marriage, how to be a strong woman after God's heart. I still have these relationships to this day and treasure every one of them. God provided healthy mentors and friends to replace the unhealthy relationships I'd had in the past.

The day Dennis decided it was time to go to the hospital, I packed my go-bag for the last time with necessary items and the power-of-attorney papers that I always kept with me. We both knew that I would be the only one coming home. I remember standing in the driveway, watching the ambulance pull away, thinking "This can't be the plan." My husband had been very sick for several days, not able to get off the couch, not able to dress himself, not able to do anything strenuous because it hurt too much to breathe. I canceled treatments and called his oncologist who said, "I'll let the ER know you're coming." How do you even prepare for that?

We went to the hospital in the middle of the pandemic (2021) when the hospitals had limited visitors to only one person and only between certain hours. So, I was going it alone. I called our son and his wife, Dennis' kids and family, everyone else who was on the list to call. And then I was alone. My husband was struggling, physically and emotionally, but consistent in his message to me: "God's got this." I wasn't sure. I wanted to believe; I wanted to feel that peace that isn't understandable. It didn't come. I busied myself with the necessary things at hand— helping Dennis communicate his needs to the nurses and doctors and providing past medical records.

Until I got home. By myself. I knew I had friends I could call and say, "come sit with me for a bit, I'm not doing well." I also knew that I needed a conversation with God, just a lay-it-all-out-there talk. So, we had it out. Waking up the next day, I had several people call and say the same words: "God sees you."

Hardest thing I've walked through to date, watching my husband die. But it was almost glorious, too. The number of people who surrounded us was breath-taking. God provided the exact person to say the exact words at the exact time to us. My friend's daughter was in the middle of writing a song and just felt compelled to call and sing it to Dennis over the phone. The title? "It's going to be alright."

When my husband decided it was time to go to hospice, the pain meds were no longer working and the oxygen levels couldn't get high enough to sustain him, God gave me the strength to say goodbye. And then, just like a loving father would do, he provided people to help walk me down the long hallways to the hospice area. I physically felt everyone's prayers and thanked the God who held

Dennis' life and mine in His hands for being gracious to us. In just a short while, he would be celebrating with Jesus and even though I would be left here on earth to navigate through these deep waters, I also knew that God would provide. Provide whatever I needed; whatever our family needed.

"Let us then with confidence, draw near to the throne of grace, that we may receive mercy and find grace to help in time of need." Hebrews 4:16

My husband's favorite verse is below:

"Do not be anxious about anything, but in every situation, by prayer and petition, with thanksgiving, present your requests to God." Philippians 4:6

Dennis lived that out, even when his breathing became so labored that we were counting the silent spaces between breaths, but death would not come.

It was always his go-to verse; it's mine now, too. Further down in that chapter, it says:

"And my God will meet all your needs, according to the riches of His glory in Christ Jesus." Philippians 4:19

There's that "all" word again.

He is…and you will…

In the space below, write out/draw/however you want to express it, how God has provided for you spiritually. List them out so you will never forget EVEN WHEN the waters pass over and you feel like you're drowning. He will always be right there.

Prayer for Provision

Jesus, you are such a good, good Father. I know that you do "see" us and are always ready and able to provide for us. What an amazing thing to know, really understand, that you care more for us (spiritually, emotionally, physically, and financially) than any other living being on earth. If we only put our trust in you. If we step out and accept your grace and mercy. You will provide above and beyond what we ever expected or dreamed of, knowing what is good for us and in your perfect timing.

We love and worship you.

In your precious name, Amen

SECTION TWO- God is my PROTECTOR

"Even when your path takes me through the valley of deepest darkness, fear will never conquer me, for you already have! Your authority is my strength and my peace. The comfort of your love takes away my fear. I'll never be lonely, for you are near. You become my delicious feast even when my enemies dare to fight." Psalm 23:4-5 (tPt)

"The righteous person may have many troubles, BUT the Lord delivers him from them ALL." Psalm 34:19 (emphasis is mine)

Chapter Five- God is my protector physically

"Boys like girls who drive trucks" was one of the mottos in my small farming community during high school. I didn't drive a truck, but I did everything the boys did and then some. I was a part of FFA (Future Farmers of America), rode 4wheelers, went mudding in the sky high trucks, knew how to weld, gambled with the boys in the barn after farm auctions, cut pigs with the neighbor farmer, shot targets as often as possible, played poker (the tame kind with pennies), milked cows with a cute boy down the road, and rode horses (saddle optional on most days).

I was fearless regarding the words that came out of my mouth and wouldn't hesitate to throw a punch if I thought it was warranted. I, physically, landed myself in some tight spots, but I was always of the mindset that I'd be able to get out of it or convince someone to get me out. I pulled the "God card" out occasionally, but I'll get into that later in this chapter.

I was a tough chicka (probably in my own head, but isn't that where you start the bluff?) UNTIL I met my husband. He seemed to be better than me in everything. I mean, everything. We had a group of single people that played cards once a month and at the time, I was the Queen of Spades. My roommate and I could just about beat everyone. Until he came along. He could go double blind nil multiple times in a game and it really didn't matter who his partner was. I was smart enough to see the potential success in others and how their success could promote my own success. So, I surrendered the crown and made sure he was my partner any time I could. I was still the winner, although truth be told, he made me Queen again, not my playing.

Dennis also carried a .45 mag with him wherever he went. That's a big gun, but he was a big guy, so you could never see it; you just always knew he was carrying. I got my conceal and carry license, got set up with a holster that fit, and purchased a gun that was the perfect size and weight for me. I rarely carried it on my person, because he always had his and I knew he would protect me always and forever. Dennis was never afraid to pull it or concerned with the consequences, because he was always in protection mode. He never flashed it or talked about it, except with his closest friends and then only to show his newest "toy".

Back to the truck… Dennis bought a short bed, Nissan 4x4 truck the summer after the cancer diagnosis when he was in remission and still working. When I had to start taking him to treatments because he was too weak to drive, he always wanted me to take the truck which had 4-wheel drive. He was comfortable with the truck, I was not, but I drove it to make him feel safe. When he passed away, I kept the truck and sold my van, only because he felt it was the safer vehicle.

Four months after he passed, I took the truck on

a youth lake trip down to Lake of the Ozarks. It drove really nice and handled the twists and turns you find down around the lake. One steep hill had me scrambling for that "tough girl driving a truck" attitude. I slid my way to the top, dropped into a valley, and stopped at the foot of another hill that seemed to go straight up. My GPS showed water on both sides of the truck. I was clearly lost. I knew I was starting to panic so I called the youth pastor and told him I was lost and could he please help me figure this out? I've never been one to panic at small things; the ride to the top of the St. Louis arch, but not getting lost at the lake. With water surrounding me. With a steep hill in front of me. And no one could find me. I dropped a pin on my phone locator as directed from the youth pastor, but he said the young men he had sent to get me, couldn't find me. "Could you start honking your horn?"

By this time, I was in a full-blown panic attack. I had crawled out of the truck and was throwing up by the side of the dirt path, just inches from whatever water was on either side of my truck. I managed to get back in the truck and start honking the horn. Like angels, the two young men came over the top of the hill, took over the driving and ignored my mascara-covered face and wild eyes. They reassured me that I wasn't far from the youth lake house and that we'd be there quickly. I was so distraught over the ordeal that I could only collapse into the house, and it took several minutes for me to get it back together. I refused to drive the truck the rest of the trip until it was time to go home.

The truck had failed to keep me safe. And my husband wasn't there to keep me safe, either. I was really mad that neither of them could make me feel safe again.

"Whoever dwells in the shelter of the Most High will rest in the shadow of the Almighty… He will cover you with His feathers and under His wings, you will find refuge. His faithfulness will be your shield and rampart…For He will command His angels concerning you to guard you in all your ways…Because he loves me, says the Lord, I will

rescue him, I will protect him because he acknowledges my name. He will call on me and I will answer him. I will be with him in trouble, I will deliver him and honor him. With long life, I will satisfy him and show him my salvation." Psalm 91

Wow, if I'd only had that verse memorized or written out on a notecard in my truck that night. Look at these words "whoever *dwells* in the *shelter* of the Most High will *rest* in the *shadow* of the Almighty". "Dwells", active tense, in the "shelter", a place of protection, will "rest" in the "shadow of the Almighty". I felt safe because I was in the shadow of my husband. I felt sheltered by him and I could always rest in the fact that he was looking out for me, physically. That was his job, right? The scripture doesn't say "Dennis, I will cover you with my feathers and under my wings, and you provide the refuge for your wife." Those words were for me. God will protect me and rescue me…me.

Put your name in that verse where appropriate and then REST there. I still needed those angels to come over the hill and my youth pastor to send them to look for me, but the panic and fear didn't need to overcome me. Psalm 23:4 reemphasizes this: "Even when your path takes me through the valley of deepest darkness, fear will never conquer me...The comfort of your love takes away my fear."

He was watching over me, even though I was putting my trust and fear in the ability of the truck and the lack of my husband's safe place.

"My help comes from the Lord, the maker of Heaven and earth. He will not let your foot slip- He who watches over you will not slumber...the Lord is your shade... the Lord will watch over your coming and going both now and forevermore."

Psalm 121:2-8

The word "watch" is used five times in that verse. My dad is a bit of a worrier, or more like he wrestles with thoughts until they come to his understanding and even then, they tend to hedge on the pessimistic side. But when storms would come,

I always appreciated his worrying.

If a physical storm was brewing, (rain, sleet, snow, thunder and lightning, high winds, tornado threats), my dad would stay up until the storm had either passed or was no longer a threat in our area. I always knew I could go to bed with confidence that Daddy would be up watching the weather reports and would wake the family if we needed to go to shelter. It was just a given that he would be watching.

God watched me get lost on those dark lake roads, watched me hyperventilate and vomit in fear, watched the young men come to my rescue, and watched me wrestle with how unsafe I felt with Dennis no longer here on earth. He didn't slumber or think "well, I hope she finds a way out of that mess." He sent help and then gently reminded me that HE was my shelter, refuge, and fortress...my physical safety was important to Him.

In the allotted space, list the ways God has protected you physically. Let these be reminders for you. EVEN WHEN we feel unsafe physically, God has promised to go before us and prepare the way for our safety. If you can't think of anything at the moment, pray about it asking God to remind you and then come back and write it down.

Chapter Six- God is my protector relationally/emotionally

When my husband passed, we had three vehicles: a motorcycle that we had been trying to sell off and on for years (long enough that we had to keep buying new tires and batteries because it sat in the garage for so long), a minivan that I drove, and the truck. I really didn't know what to do with any of them until a close friend asked me a couple of months after the funeral how she could help in a practical way. When you first become a widow, you really don't know how to tell people how you need help.

Side note: if you're a friend of a new widow and wondering how to help, just be there. The Holy Spirit will give you direction and you'll become aware of what is needed. This friend was so gentle with me; she was the one that I would call and say,

"I don't want to be a widow." She'd respond with a quiet, "I know." She validated my feelings without trying to "make everything okay" or overwhelm me with expectations.

I didn't realize there would be all of these expectations and questions people would unknowingly ask or what type of burden I would feel to have the answers. Besides all of the decisions a widow has to make regarding the funeral, the funeral home, the cemetery (which is usually separate from the funeral home), people continued to ask me questions like:

"Are you changing churches?"

From the one that Dennis and I had called home for 15+ years? Were there too many memories for me to stay? Dennis and I had been youth ministry leaders for a good portion of our time at this church and upstairs in the youth room, on the chalkboard wall designed for students and leaders to sign their name on, I had written "Dennis and Julie forever" with a big heart around it. After a year, it's still hard to look at, not because of the love with which it was written, but that one little word "forever" is one that I may never use again. Were the memories of my husband and his friends too much for the church and I needed to start over somewhere else? Really?

"What are you going to do now?"

What was I supposed to do? Figure out how to live without my husband, that's what I was going to do.

"We are hard-pressed on every side, but not crushed. Perplexed but not in despair, persecuted but not abandoned, struck down but not destroyed."
2 Corinthians 4:8-9

Hard-pressed? Understatement. Perplexed? More like stunned, but not in despair. Definitely not abandoned. Completely struck down and blind-sided (even after three years of treatments and diagnoses, we never gave up thinking that God would cause a different outcome to happen than what did), but not destroyed. Four strong promises in 23 words; all because our hope was set on Jesus.

"So, what can I do for you from a practical

standpoint?" my friend asked. After thinking about it for a minute or so, it hit me. Her husband owned the best car dealerships in the area. We bought all of our vehicles from them: 1) because they were our friends from before we were married, and 2) they had God-honoring businesses that showed in their employees and their reputation in the community.

"I need help selling off these vehicles." I said, which started the ball rolling. Her husband was brought into the conversation, I sent him the titles of the motorcycle and van, and he asked me to bring them up to their closest dealership. With the help of some other amazing friends, I was able to get the vehicles up to the dealership.

My son was with me when we settled in with one of the salesmen and the general manager. I really didn't know how emotional I was going to be just turning over the vehicles, but there were a lot of memories in both and quite frankly, it just served to re-emphasize that this was real. If Dennis were still alive, we wouldn't be selling the motorcycle (after all, he liked being able to say that he had one!) and definitely not my van (the one who took our son to school, hauled kids to sporting events, and carried students around the city for different ministry events). But here we were, and I ended up losing it in the dealership lobby.

Bright lights shining on new cars, polished showroom floors, and a sobbing widow complete with scurrying salesmen trying to find Kleenex. They were all so attentive while I tried not to drop tears on my signature on the back of the titles. One of them took especially good care of me, bringing me water and assuring me that he would get the best deal he could for me. He was the one I had the most interaction with and the one who engaged me in safe conversation topics (I'm sure that was just as much for him as it was for me- no reason to have a repeat situation!); I saw him multiple times over the next month as he kept me informed of when the vehicles would go to auction, how the auction was going (he even let me watch the auction from his work station), to pick up the checks from the sales.

Skip forward a month or so... I started leading a

book study at church: "It's Not Supposed to be This Way" by Lysa Terkeurst. In one of the chapters, she makes a profound statement that really spoke to me in the moment. "You steer where you stare." Hmmm… where was I staring? At the gentleman who had been so kind to me at the dealership.

I started counting down the miles to the next oil change and when I would see him again. He already had my number and we'd texted back and forth about some of those safe topics we'd discussed previously, always initiated by me. I really missed the interaction, both physical and emotional, between my husband and I and this guy had been super attentive. So I started to "steer where I stared."

At one point, a close friend and my sister asked me the same question (after hearing his name several times): Is he a Christian? Where does he go to church? Well, how am I supposed to know that if I don't go out with him or at least show him I'm interested? I thought I knew the answer, but I chose to deflect instead. After all, didn't I deserve a little attention? I wouldn't step ALL the way over the line I had drawn for myself decades ago before getting married. And once I found out FOR SURE that he didn't love Jesus like I did, I'd be done. I was starting to steer a little farther over the dotted line on the road I was walking. My stare was quickly becoming an infatuation.

After my sister and friend started asking those hard questions, I was jolted back from the enemy's grasp. I almost fell into the trap of "I deserve" and "I'm just curious, it won't hurt anybody." I had made a commitment to myself when I realigned with Jesus that I wouldn't get involved with anyone who didn't love Jesus more than me. What was I thinking? The salesman at the dealership wasn't the enemy, nor is he a bad guy; he was simply kind and gentlemanly and probably a great person. But not what was best for me at that moment. I was vulnerable and raw, and Satan (my true enemy) saw my need and took advantage.

"We all experience times of testing, which is

normal for every human being. But God will be faithful to you. He will screen and filter the severity, nature, and timing of every test or trial you face so that you can bear it. And each test is an opportunity to trust him more, for along with every trial God has provided for you a way of escape that will bring you out of it victoriously."

1 Corinthians 10: 13 (tPt)

Here's my evidence of escape: in February 2022 (11 months after my husband passed away and 7 months after I sold the vehicles), I had the opportunity to go on a rewards trip with my friend's dealership employees as a travel buddy with the executive/personal assistant who had just lost her husband to cancer.

There were two shifts of employees going on the rewards trip, I went with my newly widowed friend on the first leg; the salesman mentioned above was on the second leg. God knew my steering would go astray again if we were on the same part of the trip. Instead, I got the treasure of reconnecting with my friend and allowing God to work through me as I was farther on this widow journey than she was. What an incredible avenue of escape with the added benefit of a rekindling an old friendship.

My lessons in this not-so-short story:

1) Your heart and emotions will lie to you. (Jeremiah 17:9 says "The heart is deceitful above all things, and desperately wicked; who can know it?") Satan uses your words and watches your actions, waiting for the opportunity to steal, kill, and destroy.

2) Allow and encourage your true friends to speak into your life. Allow them to hold you accountable. Listen to their words of caution and their gentle re-steering.

3) If your true friends do say something to you that you know is re-steering (but you don't like it), go to God with it ("my refuge" 2 Samuel 22:3-4, Psalm 46:1, Psalm 57:1 and countless other verses) and let Him hide you under His wings and be your shield for a bit. The re-steering will be set straight

again and you'll be reminded of how much love He has for you.

In the space below, list the ways God has protected you relationally or emotionally. Let these be reminders for you EVEN WHEN the enemy has you in his sights.

Chapter Seven- God is my protector financially

"For the love of money is the root of all evil; which while some coveted after, they have erred from the faith, and pierced themselves through with many sorrows." I Timothy 6:10

I never grew up thinking I was rich or poor; I knew there were sacrifices, or what I liked to call "exchanges" for things. We, as a family, would go out to eat, but the exchange was you could only drink water. You could buy a new car, but why not buy a new-to-you car and not have as much debt? Or when our son was ready for school, Christian education was important to us, so in order for us to be able to afford tuition, I had to go back to work. There was never a time when we could just spend money without thinking about the exchange.

For the longest time, I thought that the scripture above didn't really apply to me because I didn't love money, or so I thought. Now I think that the whole thought about "exchanges" brings new light to the next verse.

> *"For where your treasure is, there will your heart be also."* Matthew 6:21

I was just moving money around, robbing that envelope to pad this envelope because I wanted this (insert item).

> *"To all the rich of this world, I command you not to be wrapped in thoughts of pride over your prosperity, or rely on your wealth, for your riches are unreliable and nothing compared to the living God.* **Trust instead in the one who lavishes upon us all good things, fulfilling our every need.** *Remind the wealthy to be rich in remarkable works of extravagant generosity, willing to share with*

others. These spiritual investments will provide a beautiful foundation for their lives and secure for them a great future, as they lay their hands upon the meaning of true life."

I Timothy 6:17-19 (emphasis mine)

Dennis and I prayed about the big purchases, and we tithed regularly and were equally generous, but we didn't really think about being good stewards of the financial blessings we were given. During a particular sermon on financial treasures that our lead pastor shared with the church, we were instantly convicted of being good stewards of our money. Praying about the small things, too. A steward watched over all things, down to the donuts and Starbucks we got every morning. They weren't bad things, but they weren't necessary things, nor were they things God forbade us to buy. But were they the best things to spend our money on? That was the question we started asking ourselves.

After Dennis passed away, there were several financial things to take into consideration: social security, 401K, insurance, investments. While eating dinner with a couple of friends, I was once again asked, "How can we help?" I shared with them where I was in the process of sorting through all of the death paperwork and the "x, y, and z" financial records that the company my husband worked for wanted from me. A lot of it had terms I'd never heard of, much less knew what to do with, but I told my friends that our policy had been to be good stewards of anything that was given to us. The husband pointed me to the below verse and gave me a piece of advice that I will always hold on to and put with these scriptures:

"Discretion will protect you and understanding will guard you." Proverbs 2:11

He said, "Choose someone that has proven to be a good steward of the things God has given them and then pattern your financial decisions after theirs." Wow, what a thought. Pattern my decisions after someone who I respected and knew they followed after God's heart? I do that in my writing (follow the example of someone I respect and who's been published); I follow my pastor and his wife's way of relationally connecting with people; I set an example of mature Christian living for the youth that I serve in ministry. But financially? Hadn't really thought that way. So, I took his advice, prayed to God for understanding on what He wanted me to do to be financially responsible and asked for protection in being obedient.

I found someone to advise me on being a good financial steward and then took an additional step and asked him who did his taxes. I thank God regularly for Godly people in my life who are on this journey with me and for the "light on my path" that God always provides and protects.

In the space below, list the ways God has protected you financially EVEN WHEN the enemy wants to mislead you and puts shiny objects that are not gold in front of you. Let these be reminders for you.

Chapter Eight- God is my protector spiritually

"Preserve my life, bring me out of trouble, silence my enemies, destroy all my foes." Psalm 143:11-12

When I was in college, and when I was actually walking with God for a short time, I ran into a young man in our singles group that became very attentive to me. He was attractive, older, and he asked me to ride in his red Corvette. How could I refuse? I asked him to stop by my dorm room for a jacket (we were taking the t-tops off) and he kindly obliged. When I went into the bathroom to change clothes, I left him looking at my pictures and books on my desk. I came out to hear him whispering gibberish and touching my closet, my desk, my bed.

My first thought was it was a foreign language that I wasn't familiar with, but when he turned to look at me. I almost lost my standing. His normally gray-green eyes were lit up, like a slow deep burn. I knew at that moment what I had walked into; the enemy was standing in the flesh in my bedroom. I'd never seen a demon before, but I believed that this man in my dorm room was here to destroy me. And I let him in.

I was able to get away from him and ran to a friend and told her what had happened. I never saw him again, but only by the grace of God did I escape what could have been a really, really bad death sentence. My friend brought people in and we all prayed over the room, prayed that nothing was left behind or spiritually attached to anything. God protected me, even then, when I didn't know how close evil was to me.

When I worked at the prison, I encountered any and all types of evil; people who had murdered or sexually assaulted others, individuals who had little regard for life itself. The most terrifying evil was almost always the spiritual kind, when you were acutely aware of the spiritual battle raging around you. It was the stuff horror movies were made of if you didn't know there was a spiritual realm trying to claim you. If you did know about the spiritual battles, you were also very aware that you had the power to combat the evil intentions because you knew the word that made even demons shake: Jesus.

In that job, I was not walking with Jesus, but I did believe in the spiritual things of this world. I had an older inmate in my housing unit that would shave off pieces of his hair and sprinkle it in front of my office door, letting me know I was in his line of sight for all evil things. In my boldness, and stupidity, I would step over the line of hair and say a quick prayer for protection. Even then, when I wasn't under the umbrella of God's control over my life, even then he protected me.

I've had a demon roar in my face, felt the pull of chaos in a room from the spiritual battles, believe witchcraft is very real, and have experienced second-hand, the torment Satan can use to pursue people. Even then, He's always protected me because I accepted Him as Lord and Savior over my life and I had praying parents. I always knew the name of Jesus had authority and the enemy had to flee.

Sometimes, when a person first becomes a widow, the loss and grief is so deep that you aren't sure how to go on. The enemy will start to whisper things to you: "You aren't anybody now." Or "What good are you?" or "Maybe you caused this" or "You're not going to make it without …(deceased)". Even the label, "widow", feels lonely. You are vulnerable and raw and probably in a state of shock even if the death was "expected". I know I felt a lot of those things and still hear some faint whisperings, but I trust His Word who says He is faithful.

"But let all who take refuge in you be glad...spread your protection over them."
Psalm 5:11

"May the Lord answer you when you are in distress; may the name of the God of Jacob protect you." Psalm 20:1

Go to God with your thoughts; He already knows them, but He wants that type of relationship with you. And then *"be strong and courageous, do not be afraid or terrified for the Lord your God goes with you, he will never leave you or forsake you."* (Deuteronomy 31:6)

These waters are rough, I know, but it's important to allow God's protection to wash over you. Hide in His shadow while you regain His strength. Remember the part of Psalm 23 at the beginning of this chapter?

*"Even when **your** path takes me **through** the valley of deepest darkness, fear will **never conquer** me, for you already have! **Your authority** is my **strength** and my **peace**..."* Psalm 23:4 (tPt) (emphasis mine)

In the space allotted, list the ways God has protected you spiritually, EVEN WHEN the spiritual battles flow into the physical and you feel bombarded by the enemy. Let these be reminders for you.

Prayer for Protection

Jesus, you are such a good, good Father. But, I am so tired and so not alert to the things around me in the physical or spiritual realm. Protect me on all fronts while I emotionally, relationally, financially, and maybe even physically go hide in your refuge. Let me hear Your whispers through Your Word, my dearest friends, my church so that I can emerge triumphant and ready to take on the plans that you still have for me. Be the shield that guards my heart and mind and soul as I navigate these waters. Thank you for being faithful and protecting me from any fiery darts the enemy throws my way.

In your precious name, Amen

SECTION THREE-God is my PLANNER

"He offers a resting place for me in his luxurious love. His tracks take me to an oasis of peace near the quiet brook of bliss. That's where he restores and revives my life. He opens before me the right path and leads me along in his footsteps of righteousness so that I can bring honor to his name." Psalm 23:2-3

"So why would I fear the future? Only goodness and tender love pursue me all the days of my life. Then afterward, when my life is through,

I'll return to your glorious presence to be forever with you!" Psalm 23:6

Chapter Nine- God is my planner physically

When I was in middle school, I decided to be a cop. I had it clearly lined out for the rest of my days. I also wanted to be a rodeo queen and a writer. So, I would be a cop by day, write out my exploits and experiences with "characters" in the evening, and rodeo on the weekends. Oh, and throw in a handsome cowboy. Makes sense, doesn't it? For an eleven-year-old. As I grew up, my plans started changing. I had to sell my horses when I went to college so rodeoing was out. One of my horses was a Shetland pony that was no more interested in doing what I wanted than me doing what my parents wanted. Kindred spirits. The closest I came to a rodeo was showing him in small horse shows, 4-H ones that showed more of my horsemanship than his. I just had to stay topside balancing an egg on a spoon while he cantered around the arena. Neither of us were good or blue ribbon worthy. My other horse, a beautiful Appaloosa with grey/blue eyes, was trained as a trail horse so her trot (through trails and trees) was heavenly, but her gallop was treacherous. There isn't a place for trail horses in rodeos. So I made up stories about rodeos and handsome cowboys.

The cop part was still a goal all the way through high school and into college. In college, I ran around with the city and campus police, saw the good, the bad, and the ugly on the job. There were a couple of us in my dorm who were criminal justice majors and several others that I made friends with from class that would all go out and "practice". We'd drive each other around blindfolded (not the driver—that would not be safe! Sarcasm, mine. We did a lot of unsafe things.) and stop at an unknown location. The blindfolded ones would have to "call it in" (landmarks included) and then get us back to "base" (the police station). That was fun until someone got dropped off, had to find their way home in the dark, and got in trouble for being out past curfew. Or the time we thought it would be fun to go up to Lover's Lane and bang on steamy car windows. That got a little dicey as no one was supposed to be up there, including us, so the "faux police" nearly got picked up by the real cops for trespassing.

My senior year of college, I was chosen for a state highway patrol class. I thought it was cool as the assignment was to get Team A drunk and then let Team B practice their sobriety check skills. I wanted to show off what I'd learned in my classes and maybe get my foot in the door with the highway patrol. I was, of course, chosen for Team A. We had to get drunk (controlled— the HP gave us just enough alcohol to impair our vision based on our weight), drive a car through a maze (with HP in the vehicle and those training controls so they could shift the controls if we got too crazy and ran over all of the orange traffic cones), and then follow all of the sobriety check instructions. Turns out, one of my fellow classmates was a mean drunk and actually tried to hit one of the HP instructors. HP was decidedly not for me.

I went along on several ride-alongs over the years in college and quickly realized that while I had the communication skills to calm someone down, I did not have the driving skills to maneuver through people who pulled out in front of you (lights blazing and siren blaring) or in a high speed car chase. I just didn't have that in me... the adrenaline, yes. The talent, no. I supposed I could have received training, but it just became something that I didn't want to do.

Even though I had purposed in my heart that I was going to be in law enforcement, prepared for it, planned for it, it just wasn't going to happen.

"Many are the plans in the mind of man but it is the purpose of the Lord that will stand."
Proverbs 19:21

When I made up my mind to become a cop, and

when I changed my mind to not be a cop, neither time did I consult God. My "shape" of who I was becoming (my personality, talents, experiences) was starting to emerge as I pursued my plans, but it never occurred to check in with Him. The whole Bible is filled with the words "plans" and "purposes". His plans and purposes.

Isaiah 14:24 and Isaiah 46:10 both say the equivalent of He has a plan and purpose and they will stand through the generations.

"The heart of man plans his way, but the Lord establishes his steps." Proverbs 16:9

Psalm 37:23 uses the word "establish" as well. "Establish" according to the English dictionary means to "set on a firm or permanent basis". So, while I made plans to be a law-enforcing, weekend rodeo-queen, writer, God was establishing His plans for my life. He was gathering up all of the talents (or non-talents), sifting through them and preparing me for His plans. Physically, I was never meant to be a rodeo queen or a cop.

> *"Teach me to do your will. Lead me on level ground." Psalm 143:10*

I always knew that training was the key to success in almost everything you do. I knew I had the talent to be a writer, but to be a good writer, I would have to train (or learn) everything I could and apply it to my writing. I went to conferences, workshops, joined a writer's group, hung out with others that had the same desires as I did. I learned tips and was taught how to plot and characterize; added those things to my already vivid imagination and I had the makings to be an author.

Same with being a Christ-follower. I had to learn about Christ, how He did things, and how to listen and obey. There were things I needed to be taught how to do, like telling my faith journey to others, and how to be disciplined to read the Bible daily and how to listen to Him. I needed to know how to be led by Him; what that looked like, how to do that. "Lead me on level ground" is now one of my life verses; I want Him to lead me.

Psalm 32:8 says the same as Psalm 143:10 but adds "I will counsel you with my eye upon you." If God is for us (and not against us) and is willing to lead us to a firm and permanent place AND will counsel us if we start to waver or wander (like a mother with her child), how can we walk away from that?

Let's read Psalm 23:2-3 again. "He offers a *resting place* for me in his luxurious love." (v. 2a)

"*His tracks* take me to an oasis of peace near the quiet brook of bliss."(v. 2b) He has left us a trail of how to follow Him.

"That's where he *restores* and *revives* my life." (v. 3a) That's what I want, restoration and revival.

"He *opens* before me the *right path* and *leads me along* in *his footsteps* of righteousness..." (v. 3b)

I never wanted to be a widow. I said that in an earlier chapter and I meant it; nobody does. It wasn't in my plans. I didn't get married with the thought that I would be a widow.

"But as it is written, 'what no eye has seen, nor ear heard nor the heart of man imagined, what God has prepared for those who love Him." I

Corinthians 2:9

So, God did plan for me to be a widow? How can I even process that? And yet... here I am. Telling you that God's plans and purposes are settled and that He would never lead you astray or abandon you. Hard words to comprehend. As I sit here writing (the plan that He birthed in me that I actually am doing), it occurred to me (see? You get to discover this journey of being led and following His tracks with me), that maybe, just maybe, He was preparing ME for "such a time as this."

In the space below, list the ways God has fulfilled plans for you physically EVEN WHEN they weren't the plans you had in mind. Let these be reminders for you.

Chapter Ten- God is my planner relationally/emotionally

I'm a planner by nature. I love lists and getting a new planner every year. I have ten different "to do" lists on my phone, my planner holds everything from calendar items to more "to do" lists to lists of authors I want to read to a sketch of my flower garden (so I know what flowers I already have and what I can buy for fillers). I've planned small things like birthday parties to big things like youth conferences with almost 1,000 students. I've made bad planning decisions like having a cake decorated with school colors (red and black) and having guests walk around with black teeth and I've made some really good planning decisions like planning my wedding.

I had a boss that I completely admired and

respected that was always in charge of big ministry productions. Because I was his executive assistant, I was always in on the planning. He required excellence in everything, including the staff around him. When we geared up for an event, he would write out the talking points and the flow of the schedule, much like a play script.

House lights down; center spotlight up.

Guest speaker will enter the stage from the right: "speech here" which has been reviewed 1.5 weeks prior to the event.

Cue band on the last word of speech "Thank you all for attending…"

It was all choreography beautifully and practiced at least once with all of the moving parts involved.

I pattern the events I lead out in the same way. I loved the structure and the care and forethought that was noticeable when planned that way. "Flying by the seat of your pants" was not an option for me. Dennis could "wing it", but he didn't have the same experiences or training that I had.

I recently led a book study in a small group at church and I always planned out how the meetings would go with backup plans, if needed. It was like a small-scale coding exercise.

6:30pm Opening Prayer

6:35pm Icebreaker Activity (unless too few participants and then go to #3)

6:45pm Show video clip (cue up before study)

7:15pm Discuss author's talking points #2, #7, #8

7:35pm Ask the group if they'd like to share anything they learned from the video or assigned book chapters

7:45pm Prayer Requests

"Wait, you want to go back to the questions that we already discussed at 7:15pm? But, the schedule says we should be doing prayer requests right now. We only have five minutes, so you have to be fast." These were the thoughts in my head as I watched the tears build up speed on this young woman's face. I had planned with the best intentions, but left the Holy Spirit out of the occasion. In this hurry up and go to the next thing, we often leave out the relational planning. When I realized what I had done, we stopped everything and spent time ministering to her as she poured out the things that God had revealed to her through the study. Most events can operate on a schedule and be planned out to the smallest details, but in ministry work, you have to be ready for the Holy Spirit to take you in a different direction.

As I mentioned in the last chapter, I had plans to be a law enforcement officer for most of my high school and college days. When that plan didn't seem feasible, I accepted a position as a case manager at a medium security correctional facility. After four years, I walked away from that job and started working at a day reporting center for juveniles which morphed into working with juvenile offenders. I discovered that I really liked teenagers, the hard ones that smoked pot and lived in their car, also the ones that had been given a crappy poker hand or were suicidal. I loved meeting them where they were at, emotionally, and working with them to find a decent physical home. That job was connected to the state operating procedures so I was limited in how much I could really work with them, handcuffed to policies on how much I could say or do.

Fast forward another four years, my husband and I both volunteered to work with the youth of our church.

"The Lord will fulfill His purpose for me…"
Psalm 138:8

Little did I know that I would continue in youth ministry for the next 25 years. I also substituted at the Christian school where my son attended, and my favorite classes were with the secondary students (6th-12th grade). I've developed a pattern: I was a teenager once, I worked with juvenile offenders and middle/high school students, and now I'm in youth ministry. In each of those roles, you couldn't have told me that this was the plan for my life, to relate and minister to youth. I already had a plan for my life; did I feel circumvented? No, because as God allowed me to experience all of these roles, He grew a deep love for teenagers to emerge at the same pace. His purpose for my life is right where I am.

"And we know that for those who love God all things work together for good for those who are called according to His purpose." Romans 8:28

When I stepped back into my rightful spot and rededicated my life to God, He continued in the plan that He always had for me- to relate to teenagers. I love to watch them grow and mature in their faith. I love to watch them struggle with God and wrestle through the decision to make their relationship with Him their own. I love to watch others with my same desire pour out love on them. I love to watch the plan for their life unfold.

I had a young woman approach me at a funeral of a friend and she said, "you may not remember me, but I was in the youth group with you and I just want to say how much I appreciated you during those years." She went on to tell me about her kids and how life was for her now. I did remember her and was stunned to hear her speak her appreciation of me as she was one of the tough kids who I was constantly on for talking or sitting on the boys' laps or sleeping during service. Even when we don't realize it, we are relating to people and contributing to the plan God has for them.

On a relational level, being a widow is very confusing. You're not really married anymore (people are quick to question that on the day that you put your wedding rings away and aren't wearing them) and "single" doesn't seem to define you either. So, after almost 24 years of marriage, I should be good with my friend base and call it good regarding future relationships? Was that the plan for me personally? I'm pretty independent and "don't need" someone to be my other half. But as a widow, and especially if your marriage was a good one, the intimacy factor is just gone.

There's no one to stick my cold feet under at night, talk to after work, share your disappointments and accomplishments with, hold hands with even through the arguments. It's just done. So many of my widowed friends have moved into new relationships and while I think that's wonderful for them, I question what God has planned for me in this chapter. My son and I talked about me dating again (how hard is that at 54 years old?) when we celebrated the one-year anniversary of Dennis' death. "I don't really know" was my response. I don't see myself being alone for the rest of my days, but I also am not ready for a relationship. So, I do what I know...I seek God for His plan and purpose for my life.

"Without counsel, plans fail, but with many advisors, they succeed." Proverbs 15:22

In my seeking, I've learned that having good advisors is pertinent. Good ones that have Godly values and my best interest at heart. People who have been through similar situations (like being a widow) and those who haven't but have different life experiences than I do and can see paths with a different perspective. When I went back to work after the funeral, there was a box on my chair.

I was later told by the person who gave it to me that it was a widow's box. It was traditional in her family to give a care package, of sorts, from one widow to another. I was overwhelmed; there were candles and bath soaps and a book about Heaven and several other special things that she wanted me to have. I was so touched by the things in the box, but even more so, by her friendship and wisdom and care for me as a new widow.

Anyone in my close friend base knows that I treasure their advice and wisdom. I take their words to heart and appreciate them speaking into my life, because I know they have been placed in my life for a reason. Above all, God's truth reigns supreme, but I know that He speaks through those closest to us, too. I have no problem asking for their wisdom and counsel and if it lines up with the truth of God, then so be it. Heed their words, even when they are hard words spoken in love.

"And which of you by being anxious, can add a single hour to his span of life?" Matthew 6:27

Uncertainty and off-script events can trigger a planner at heart to be anxious about the future. When my husband was in hospice and the nurse on duty would come in and say "it won't be long now", I, in my feeble attempt to control the situation would just nod and plan my next steps. At one point, the nurse suggested that I go home and take a shower; she said sometimes the person on death's door was waiting to pass until their loved one had left for the day.

An act of love, she said, so the loved one wouldn't have to see the death. The kids and I had already said our goodbyes. I even called my pastor and asked if I was wrong in praying for life's release so he'd be out of pain and on with Jesus. Maybe I could control that by leaving? My anxious feelings were at an all-time high, because we knew we were at the end, and I had no idea what to do. I went as far as my truck down in the parking lot and then returned in tears. By being anxious, I couldn't add to his life or speed up the process. He was in God's hands and His timing would be perfect, as perfect as the death of a loved one could be.

And so on March 13, 2021 at 11:06am, the plans and purposes for Dennis were fulfilled as he went to be with Jesus. That left me to discover the plans and purposes God still has in mind for me.

EVEN WHEN your expectations of people go awry and your intentions are misconstrued, God is on the lookout and promises to "lead you on level ground" (Psalm 143:10) in your relationships with others. In the space below, list the ways God has fulfilled plans for you relationally or emotionally. Let these be reminders for you.

Chapter Eleven- God is my planner financially

I know how to budget, how to write out a plan to stretch those dollars between paychecks or to save for items that I really wanted. Remember, I'm a list person so writing out a budget was not much different than making a list of expenses and income and hoping that the last number was in black and not red. I knew how to do all of that with my money. Throw in a husband who was a spender, quality and quantity were equal, who made three times what I did, and had things I could only imagine (investments, stocks, two ex-wives, an old bankruptcy) and a love for anything unique or collectible. I penny-pinched, writing down to the cent each grocery item so I'd have enough money in my wallet at the cashier. He had money to spend on quality and unique things.

Starting around November, I would begin listening to his "wants" so I could get the perfect Christmas gift. If I found it, I would buy it on sale and stash it somewhere in the house. In the weeks leading up to Christmas, he would inevitably find the same item with a better sale price and better attachments or bonus bucks or warranties. I would yell at him (in love, of course) and take back the one I had bought and look for something else to buy him. It drove me crazy. My presents from him were equally as frustrating, not because of what they were, but because he knew what I wanted, would go out on Christmas Eve, find it, buy it, and wrap it in a trash bag. Boom, he was done with time to spare. Side note: Most guys like shopping this way with the whole "hunt and find" mentality. I wrestled with the gift, how much to spend, how pretty it looked all wrapped up. I learned to just give him money and let him "hunt and find" what he wanted.

When we got married, we thought it best to go through a Dave Ramsey study and figure out how to combine our incomes and spending habits. So, we did, watching the videos and learning how to become financial partners in our marriage. We tried the envelope system, tried paying off the small bills first (the snowball effect), tried to round up the expenditures in the check register so there was really more pennies in the account.

In the later years of our marriage, I started recognizing the signs of a big purchase stirring in his mind and would prepare myself for the "conversation". We had agreed to talk about big purchases before actually purchasing those items and sometimes it worked, sometimes we just disagreed. The experts say that most of marriage problems come from some type of financial decision(s). I agree; it takes a lot of conversations and awareness to stay in front of that mountain.

When Dennis died and even though I was handling all of the bills, there were still things I knew nothing about. One evening while eating dinner with different friends than the ones who initially gave me the financial steward talk, the husband said to me "you know that's what I do for a living—help people manage their money." Hmmm... sounded like wise counsel was sitting at the dinner table with me.

"Your word is a lamp unto my feet, a light on my path." Psalm 119:5

I had talked to others that I trusted about my finances like my parents and some faithful friends that my husband had talked with about financial business and who gave him very sound advice. But the finances were just sitting there still. When my friend mentioned that he was willing to talk to me about my next financial steps, all I could think of was his wise counsel was the light for my path that had previously been dark and shadow-y. How like God to cause our paths to cross at just this moment.

"Trust in the Lord with all your heart and lean not on your own understanding: in all your ways, submit to Him and He will make your paths

straight." Proverbs 3:5-6

Trust is such a hard thing, because people are messy. They've made messy decisions with messy consequences. But the Lord hasn't. I don't know why I'm a widow, but Jesus does and I have to trust Him with everything even when the understanding of it all is murky and unclear. "In all your ways"- that meant my finances, too. So, we opened all of the books and prayed that God would direct my path to trust and be obedient and that my financial advisor (and friend and Christ-follower himself) would direct his decisions and bless his household. I pray every day for him as he is a good steward of my money and countless others who trust him.

In the space below, list the ways God has fulfilled plans for you financially EVEN WHEN your plans seem to bottom out. Let these be reminders for you.

Chapter Twelve- God is my planner spiritually

"The plans of the Lord stand firm forever, His purposes of His heart through all generations."
Psalm 33:11

"For we are His workmanship, created in Christ Jesus for good works which God prepared beforehand that we should walk in them."
Ephesians 2:10

*"**Before** I formed you in the womb, I knew you…" Jeremiah 1:5 (emphasis mine)*

In an earlier chapter, I mentioned how much I now disliked the word "forever". Nothing in this world is forever. Let me retract that statement; only Jesus, God, and the Holy Spirit are forever. When I was born, my dad was in Vietnam in the Marines. I'm certain that while they were looking forward to having a family, they didn't anticipate the Vietnam war and the arrival of their first child coinciding. But God did.

I suspect that they also didn't plan on me being an angry, rebellious teenager, either. But God did. Where the desire to become a law enforcement officer came from is anybody's guess because no one in the family was in law enforcement. But God did; He put those desires in my heart and soul and I fleshed them out by trial and stupidity.

When I walked away from my faith foundation, God already knew it would happen, allowed it to happen as I made my own willful decisions. He created me and knit all of those things together: my bad (and good) decisions, my desire to help people, my love for justice, my physical abilities (and challenges), and my relationships. Long before I was created. He tucked all of those things into me, Julie, and created me for future things that He had already established. He's done that for every single person.

"...for good works which God **prepared beforehand** that we should walk in them." There are a lot of theological thoughts on what "good works" we are created for, but suffice it to say that good works don't equal salvation. It can never be earned. And how "we should walk in them" is explained in a different verse (see below), but the "prepared beforehand" really caught my attention. So, if I take a dry erase board and fill it with experiences, it would look like this:

Rebellious teenager to

Works in a prison to

Works with juvenile offenders to

Works in student ministry at church

And God knew that *before* I was born.

"Call to me and I will answer you and tell you great and unsearchable things you do not know."

Jeremiah 33:3

"But the helper, the Holy Spirit, whom the

Father will send in my name, He will teach you all things and bring to your remembrance all that I have said to you." John 14:26

So, instead of fumbling around, making decisions with my limited knowledge and trying to answer the questions "Why am I still here?" or "I don't know who I am or my purpose", I'm going to call on the God who created me. What do you want me to do with my life? What are the plans you have for me? How can I honor you while you help me figure this out? If He knew all of these things before I landed in my parents' arms, He also knows my future and all I really need to do is sit tight, call on Him, and wait for Him to shed light on the next thing.

"For still the vision awaits its appointed time, it hastens to the end— it will not lie. If it seems slow, wait for it; it will surely come. It will not delay."
Habukkuk 2:3

I always receive a word from God that I return to all throughout the year. In January 2018, the word was, "Choose". That was the year we first received the cancer diagnosis (in March). I thought, wow, not the word from the Lord I was expecting, but it became clearer as the year progressed. Choose how you will respond to this diagnosis. Choose what you will stand on when the days get dark. Choose who you will call on when the times look bleak, fear or Me? In 2019, the word was "Joy"; yeah, a happy word! During the brief respite from cancer treatments, we were joyful, or maybe happy, because joy goes so much deeper and doesn't rely on fleeting feelings. Joy was what I had to dig out when the cancer came back.

In 2022, the word from the Lord is "positioning". I fully believe people, me included, are being positioned for what's to come. I believe babies are being brought into this world at this time because He has created in them the ability to lead this world. My son's generation (Gen Z) are now in their 20's because His plan is unfolding, and they need to be of an age where they can be influencers.

Someone said this generation was "born for the storm" because of the way they think and act and develop and discover what God created in them. I believe people are being positioned in government, in schools, in churches, and families. I believe in each of us, people are being positioned in our lives, causes are being put in front of us, and decisions are being made to create a new and different world, both for the good and the bad. And the spiritual battle rages on, despite the enemy knowing that he loses in the end. The vision before us, includes the plan He has for each of us as He positions us. The victory will come in the perfect timing as that's the only way God works.

In the allotted space, list the ways God has fulfilled plans for you spiritually EVEN WHEN you couldn't see it at the time. EVEN WHEN the spiritual battle continues to rage for your soul and heart and mind, let these be reminders for you.

Prayer for the Planning

Jesus, you are a good, good Father. You say in your word "For I know the plans I have for you...plans to prosper you and not to harm you, plans to give you hope and a future" (Jeremiah 29:11) and I am so thankful that you knew me before I was ever born and that you have plans for me. You know the plan for my life and although I'm eager to see that unfold, I will call on you to help me discover them and will wait while you position my days and relationships. Thank you for having the vision for me and I trust you to fulfill those plans in your timing. Help me to walk on level ground and be patient. Help me to discover my purpose and to not be afraid to step into those plans. Thank you for always going before me, behind me, and beside me.

In your precious name, Amen.

In conclusion, I want to go back to the verses we started with in Psalm 23. The words in italics are from the Passion translation (tPt); the words in parenthesis are from the New International Version (NIV).

v. 1 *Yahweh is my best friend and my shepherd. I always have more than enough. (The Lord is my shepherd, I lack nothing.)* As a widow, the thought always comes up "What now?" Your best friend never left you and will provide for you in the coming days.

v. 2 *He offers a resting place for me in his luxurious love. His tracks take me to an oasis of peace near the quiet brook of bliss. (He makes me lie down in green pastures, he leads me beside quiet waters.)* If I follow His tracks and His leading, I will recognize the places where rest is available and where I can quiet my soul.

v. 3 *That's where he restores and revives my life. He opens before me the right path and leads me along in his footsteps of righteousness so that I can bring honor to his name. (He refreshes my soul. He guides me along the right paths for His name's sake.)* I want to find that purpose for my life that is me exclusively, aside from what it was with my husband. The reason for me, now. After a time of refreshing, I believe the paths will be clear or at least I will know there is a path prepared for me in this chapter of my life. One that continues to honor Him.

v. 4 Even when your path takes me through the valley of deepest darkness, fear will never conquer me, for you already have! Your authority is my strength and my peace. The comfort of your love takes away my fear. I'll never be lonely, for you are near. (Even though I walk through the darkest valley, I will fear no evil, for you are with me; your rod and your staff, they comfort me.) I know that the refreshing time will come, but I also know that there may be dark days ahead, ones that it will be harder to walk through and where the sadness seems overwhelming. When those days come, and He said they would, I can turn to Jesus and He will be the strength I need just at the right moment. He will hide me under His wings as promised. Just as the shepherd protects the flock with his staff and leads them to protective pastures, so will Jesus.

v. 5 You become my delicious feast even when my enemies dare to fight. You anoint me with the fragrance of your Holy Spirit; you give me all I can drink of you until my cup overflows. (You prepare a table before me in the presence of my enemies. You anoint my head with oil; my cup overflows.) The enemy of my soul will be watching for weakness, where he can ensnare me in depression or sin. But my God says that He will prepare a seat at His table for me despite enemy engagement and that I can rest in that place until my strength overflows through Him.

v. 6 So why would I fear the future? Only goodness and tender love pursue me all the days of my life. Then afterward, when my life is through, I'll return to your glorious presence to be forever with you! (Surely your goodness and love will follow me all the days of my life, and I will dwell in the house of the Lord forever.) Just like the flowers of the field, I have nothing to fear about what is to come; not because He makes it easy, but because He is walking with me.

In His faithfulness, He's promised to never leave us, guide us on the right path, stave off the enemies, provide everything we need and casts all fear and concern away. That's the faithfulness I want to portray back to Him.

When the hymn "It is Well" was written by Horatio Spafford, it was after he had experienced such a great loss with all four of his daughters drowning in their passage to America. The song vibrates in my head any time the sadness kicks in, because EVEN WHEN my feelings are low and the circumstances are bleak, MY SOUL IS WELL. The saving grace of His love and His constant care, protection, and guidance supersedes it all. I've gone from knowing all of these things to leaning on His promises as He provides, protects, and plans my future. You can, too.

EVEN WHEN

My Prayer for You

Jesus, you are a good, good Father. I thank you for continually showing me the way that honors you. I thank you for the time you've carved out for me to write this book. I pray for those reading these words that may be in a bad place right now and those who are grieving the loss of their loved one and for those who may be in a good place but need the reminders of truth given throughout this book. As each reader reaches out their hands to you, I pray that you will comfort them as you have comforted me and that you will be their best friend and their Lord. That they will lean not on their own understanding, but will lean into You. May they find rest, peace, and quiet for their soul, EVEN WHEN.

Julie Brown became a widow in March 2021 and has firsthand knowledge of how grief and loss can be an all-consuming, hard journey. Julie lives in Kansas City, Missouri, with two big dogs and a penchant for writing on her back deck where hummingbirds visit, the coffee is sweet, and friends are welcomed.

Made in the USA
Coppell, TX
22 January 2023